99¢ RECIPES

Appetizers & Entrées

Eating Well.
Spending Less.

With a growing number of people feeling the pinch of tightening budgets, eating out and convenience cooking can be a financial drain. Fortunately, home-cooked meals are often more delicious and better for you than processed foods. Rediscover the pleasure of cooking at home with this collection of budget-friendly appetizer and entrée recipes that will help you eat well and save money.

DOING THE MATH

Every recipe in this collection was individually priced to determine the cost per serving. Keep in mind that food costs vary regionally and seasonally, so exact prices per serving are not included. For budget planning, each recipe is marked with either the 99¢ or Less icon or the Budget Friendly icon next to the recipe title.

 Per serving, this recipe does not cost more than 99¢ to make.

 Per serving, this recipe does not cost more than $1.99 to make.

- All calculations are based on actual grocery store prices. The least expensive ingredients available were chosen, including some store-brand products and sale items.

- Prices include all ingredients as listed in the recipe, except salt, pepper and ingredients labeled as "optional."

- If a range is offered for the amount of an ingredient (¹/₈ teaspoon to ¹/₄ teaspoon, for example), the smaller amount was used to calculate the cost per serving.

- If an ingredient is presented with an option (³/₄ cup chopped tomatoes or red bell peppers, for example), the first item listed was used to calculate the cost per serving.

- If there is a range of serving sizes (makes 4 to 6 servings, for example), the larger number of servings was used to calculate the cost per serving.

- Food shown in the photo that is not listed as an ingredient (including garnishes, optional items and serving suggestions) was not included in the cost per serving.

Shop Smart

Keep food costs from getting out of hand with these simple money-saving techniques.

Check the Sales

Take advantage of sales! Read the weekly grocery store ads before you go shopping. Or, check the website of your favorite supermarket. Many supermarkets let you review the weekly sales flyer online and create a shopping list at the same time. Sign up for e-newsletters—another helpful tool in hunting for food bargains.

Make a List

Make a grocery list before you go shopping. It will get you out of the store faster, and it will also prevent you from spending money on things you don't need.

Use Coupons

Coupons do count! Find coupons in newspaper ads, supermarket flyers or with your grocery receipts. Also, look for printable coupons on food manufacturers' and supermarkets' websites. Keep them in a convenient place so they are always with you when you go shopping. Saving pennies adds up.

Take Advantage of Volume Discounts

Discounted pricing is sometimes available when you buy a full case or larger quantities. For example, buy family-size packages of meat, divide them into meal-sized portions and freeze for future meals. However, when buying in large package sizes, be sure to compare the unit pricing to determine which size of a product is the best value. The biggest package is not always the best value.

Go Generic

Most major supermarket chains have introduced house brands. The savings can be considerable when purchasing a generic-labeled product instead of a brand-name one.

Cooking more meals at home is a huge step in the right direction to stretch your food dollar. With smart grocery shopping and the recipes in this book, your family can actually eat better while you save money.

Affordable Appetizers

99¢ or LESS | Mediterranean Flatbread

2 tablespoons olive oil, divided
½ cup thinly sliced yellow onion
½ cup thinly sliced red bell pepper
½ cup thinly sliced green bell pepper
1 package (11 ounces) refrigerated French bread dough
2 cloves garlic, minced
½ teaspoon dried rosemary
⅛ teaspoon red pepper flakes (optional)
⅓ cup chopped pitted ripe or kalamata olives
¼ cup grated Parmesan cheese

1. Preheat oven to 350°F.

2. Heat 1 tablespoon oil in large skillet over medium-high heat. Add onion and bell peppers; cook and stir 5 minutes or until onion begins to brown. Remove from heat.

3. Unroll dough on nonstick baking sheet. Combine garlic and remaining 1 tablespoon oil in small bowl; spread evenly over dough. Sprinkle with rosemary and red pepper flakes, if desired. Top with onion mixture; sprinkle with olives.

4. Bake 16 to 18 minutes or until golden brown. Sprinkle with cheese. Cool on wire rack. Cut flatbread in half lengthwise; cut crosswise into 1-inch-wide strips. *Makes 16 pieces (2 per serving)*

Festive Taco Cups

1 tablespoon vegetable oil
½ cup chopped onion
½ pound ground turkey or ground beef
1 clove garlic, minced
½ teaspoon dried oregano
½ teaspoon chili powder or taco seasoning
¼ teaspoon salt
1¼ cups (5 ounces) shredded taco cheese blend or Mexican cheese blend, divided
1 can (11½ ounces) refrigerated breadstick dough
Chopped fresh tomato and sliced green onion (optional)

1. Heat oil in large skillet over medium heat. Add onion; cook and stir until tender. Add turkey; cook until turkey is no longer pink, stirring to break up meat. Stir in garlic, oregano, chili powder and salt. Remove from heat and stir in ½ cup cheese; set aside.

2. Preheat oven to 375°F. Lightly grease 36 mini (1¾-inch) muffin cups. Remove dough from container but do not unroll dough. Separate dough into 8 pieces at perforations. Divide each piece into 3 pieces; roll or pat each piece into 3-inch circle. Press circles into prepared muffin cups.

3. Fill each cup with 1½ to 2 teaspoons turkey mixture. Bake 10 minutes. Sprinkle tops of taco cups with remaining ¾ cup cheese; bake 2 to 3 minutes more or until cheese is melted. Garnish with tomato and green onion, if desired.

Makes 36 taco cups (3 per serving)

99¢ or LESS | # Honey-Mustard Chicken Wings

3 pounds chicken wings
1 teaspoon salt
1 teaspoon black pepper
½ cup honey
½ cup barbecue sauce
2 tablespoons spicy brown mustard
1 clove garlic, minced
3 to 4 thin lemon slices

Slow Cooker Directions

1. Cut off chicken wing tips; discard. Cut each wing at joint to make two pieces. Sprinkle wing pieces with salt and pepper; place on broiler rack. Broil 4 to 5 inches from heat about 10 minutes, turning halfway through cooking time. Place in slow cooker.

2. Combine honey, barbecue sauce, mustard and garlic in small bowl; mix well. Pour sauce over chicken wings. Top with lemon slices. Cover; cook on LOW 4 to 5 hours.

3. Remove and discard lemon slices. Serve wings with sauce.

Makes about 24 wings (2 per serving)

 tip | Whole chicken wings have three sections. The wing tips are usually cut off and discarded or frozen for making stock. The remaining piece is cut apart at the joint to make 2 wings. Chicken wings are sometimes sold as drummettes, which look like miniature drumsticks.

 **Party Mix**

3 cups bite-size rice cereal squares
2 cups toasted oat ring cereal
2 cups bite-size wheat cereal squares
1 cup peanuts or pistachio nuts
1 cup thin pretzel sticks
½ cup (1 stick) butter, melted
1 tablespoon Worcestershire sauce
1 teaspoon seasoned salt
½ teaspoon garlic powder
⅛ teaspoon ground red pepper (optional)

Slow Cooker Directions

1. Combine cereals, nuts and pretzels in slow cooker.

2. Mix butter, Worcestershire sauce, seasoned salt, garlic powder and red pepper, if desired, in small bowl. Pour over cereal mixture in slow cooker; toss lightly to coat.

3. Cover; cook on LOW 3 hours, stirring well every 30 minutes. Cook, uncovered, 30 minutes more. Store cooled party mix in airtight container.   *Makes 10 (1-cup) servings*

Note: Create a custom mix to fit your taste. Just substitute your favorite unsweetened cereals for any of the above cereals.

 Keep homemade snack mixes on hand for parties and munching. Homemade mixes are easy to prepare and are much cheaper and healthier than prepared snacks.

Spinach, Crab and Artichoke Dip

1 package (10 ounces) frozen chopped spinach, thawed
   and squeezed dry
1 package (8 ounces) cream cheese
1 jar (about 7 ounces) marinated artichoke hearts, drained
   and finely chopped
1 can (6½ ounces) crabmeat, drained and shredded
¼ teaspoon hot pepper sauce
Melba toast or whole grain crackers (optional)

Slow Cooker Directions

1. Combine spinach, cream cheese, artichoke hearts, crabmeat and hot pepper sauce in 1½-quart slow cooker.

2. Cover; cook on HIGH 1½ to 2 hours or until heated through, stirring after 1 hour. (Dip will stay warm in slow cooker for 2 hours.)

3. Serve with melba toast, if desired.   *Makes 10 (¼-cup) servings*

 Frozen spinach is cheaper than fresh spinach. When on special, purchase extra packages to keep in the freezer for dips, soups and casseroles.

 **Chipotle Orange BBQ Drumsticks**

½ cup barbecue sauce, preferably mesquite or hickory smoked

1 to 2 tablespoons minced canned chipotle peppers in adobo sauce

1 teaspoon grated orange peel

8 skinless chicken drumsticks

1 teaspoon ground cumin

1. Spray grill grid with nonstick cooking spray. Prepare grill for direct cooking.

2. Combine barbecue sauce, chipotle peppers and orange peel in small bowl. Set aside.

3. Sprinkle drumsticks evenly with cumin.

4. Grill chicken, covered, over medium heat 30 to 35 minutes or until cooked through (165°F), turning frequently. Baste with sauce during last 5 minutes, turning and basting until all of sauce is used.

Makes 4 servings (2 drumsticks per serving)

 Chicken drumsticks are a great value. Since they contain more fat than white meat, they are ideal for grilling. Although drumsticks take a little longer to cook, they stay moist and tender on the grill. Turn frequently for even cooking. To test for doneness, a fork should insert easily and the juices should be clear.

Micro Mini Stuffed Potatoes

99¢ or LESS

1 pound small new potatoes, scrubbed
¼ cup sour cream
2 tablespoons butter, softened
½ teaspoon minced garlic
¼ cup milk
½ cup (2 ounces) shredded sharp Cheddar cheese
½ teaspoon salt
¼ teaspoon black pepper
¼ cup finely chopped green onions (optional)

1. Pierce potatoes with fork in several places. Microwave potatoes on HIGH 5 to 6 minutes or until tender. Let stand 5 minutes; cut in half lengthwise. Scoop out pulp from potatoes and place in medium bowl.

2. Beat potato pulp with electric mixer at low speed 30 seconds. Add sour cream, butter and garlic; beat until well blended. Gradually add milk, beating until smooth. Add cheese, salt and pepper; beat until blended.

3. Fill each potato shell with equal amounts of potato mixture. Microwave on HIGH 1 to 2 minutes or just until cheese melts. Garnish with green onions, if desired.

Makes 4 servings (2 potatoes per serving)

Note: Small russet potatoes can be substituted for the new potatoes.

 tip

Micro-bake potatoes when in a hurry to get a meal on the table. Scrub and pierce the potatoes in several places with a fork. Microwave on HIGH for 5 to 7 minutes or until the potatoes feel soft when gently squeezed. Let the potatoes stand about 5 minutes for a better texture.

Firecracker Black Bean Dip

1 can (16 ounces) refried black beans
¾ cup salsa
2 jalapeño peppers,* seeded and minced
1 teaspoon chili powder
½ cup crumbled queso fresco**
3 green onions, sliced
   Tortilla chips (optional)
   Assorted cut-up vegetables (optional)

*Jalapeño peppers can sting and irritate the skin, so wear rubber gloves when handling peppers and do not touch your eyes.

**Queso fresco is a mild white Mexican cheese. If unavailable, you may substitute shredded Monterey Jack or Cheddar cheese.

Slow Cooker Directions

1. Combine beans, salsa, peppers and chili powder in 2-quart slow cooker. Cover; cook on LOW 3 to 4 hours or on HIGH 2 hours.

2. Top with queso fresco and green onions. Serve warm with tortilla chips and vegetables, if desired. *Makes 8 servings*

 Canned beans are inexpensive but much more expensive than dried beans. Although cooking beans takes time, you can save money by cooking a larger quantity of beans than are needed for one recipe. Freeze the remainder of the beans with some cooking liquid in individual containers. They will keep for several months in the freezer. To use, thaw in the refrigerator or microwave.

Soups & Stews

Double Corn Chowder

2 stalks celery, chopped

6 ounces chopped ham

1 small onion or 1 large shallot, chopped

1 jalapeño pepper,* seeded and minced

1 cup frozen corn, thawed

1 cup canned hominy

¼ teaspoon salt

¼ teaspoon dried thyme

¼ teaspoon black pepper

1 cup chicken broth

1 tablespoon all-purpose flour

1½ cups milk, divided

*Jalapeño peppers can sting and irritate the skin, so wear rubber gloves when handling peppers and do not touch your eyes.

Slow Cooker Directions

1. Combine celery, ham, onion, jalapeño, corn, hominy, salt, thyme and black pepper in 4-quart slow cooker. Add broth. Cover; cook on LOW 5 to 6 hours or on HIGH 3 to 3½ hours.

2. Blend flour and 2 tablespoons milk in small bowl. Stir into corn mixture. Add remaining milk. Cover; cook on LOW 20 minutes or until slightly thickened and heated through. *Makes 4 servings*

99¢ or LESS | Chili Mac in the Slow Cooker

1 pound ground beef or turkey
½ cup chopped onion
1 can (about 14 ounces) diced tomatoes, drained
1 can (8 ounces) tomato sauce
1 packet (1 ounce) chili seasoning
¼ teaspoon red pepper flakes (optional)
¼ teaspoon black pepper
8 ounces uncooked elbow macaroni
Shredded Cheddar cheese (optional)

Slow Cooker Directions

1. Brown beef and onion 6 to 8 minutes in large skillet over medium heat, stirring to break up meat. Drain fat.

2. Place beef mixture, tomatoes, tomato sauce, chili seasoning, red pepper flakes, if desired, and black pepper in slow cooker; mix well. Cover; cook on LOW 4 hours.

3. Cook macaroni according to package directions until al dente; drain. Add macaroni to slow cooker; mix well. Cover; cook on LOW 1 hour. Serve with cheese, if desired. *Makes 4 to 6 servings*

 tip | When shopping for ground beef, check the price per pound on each package size. Ground beef packed in 5 pound chubs or large family packs often costs less per pound than smaller packages.

Split Pea Soup

1 package (16 ounces) dried green or yellow split peas
4 ounces smoked sausage links, sliced and quartered
5 cups water
1 can (about 14 ounces) chicken broth
1 medium onion, chopped
2 medium carrots, chopped
½ teaspoon dried basil
¼ teaspoon dried oregano
¼ teaspoon black pepper

1. Rinse peas thoroughly in colander under cold running water, discarding any debris or blemished peas.

2. Combine peas, sausage, water, broth, onion, carrots, basil, oregano and pepper in Dutch oven. Bring to a boil over high heat. Reduce heat to medium-low; simmer, uncovered, 1 hour 15 minutes or until peas are tender, stirring occasionally. Stir frequently near end of cooking to keep soup from scorching. Cool slightly.

3. Transfer sausage to plate. Place 3 cups soup in food processor or blender; process until smooth.

4. Return puréed soup and sausage to Dutch oven. If soup is too thick, add water until desired consistency is reached. Heat through.

Makes 6 servings

 Split peas are very economical and easy to prepare because they do not require soaking. Salt the peas, if desired, after they are cooked. Salt in the cooking liquid slows down the cooking and toughens the peas.

Lentil Stew over Couscous

3 cups dried lentils (1 pound), sorted and rinsed
3 cups water
1 can (about 14 ounces) chicken broth
1 can (about 14 ounces) diced tomatoes
1 large onion, chopped
1 green bell pepper, chopped
2 stalks celery, chopped
1 medium carrot, halved lengthwise and sliced
2 cloves garlic, chopped
1 teaspoon dried marjoram
¼ teaspoon black pepper
1 tablespoon olive oil
1 tablespoon cider vinegar
4½ to 5 cups hot cooked couscous

Slow Cooker Directions

1. Combine lentils, water, broth, tomatoes, onion, bell pepper, celery, carrot, garlic, marjoram and black pepper in slow cooker; stir. Cover; cook on LOW 8 to 9 hours or until vegetables are tender.

2. Stir in oil and vinegar. Serve over couscous.

Makes 8 to 10 servings

tip | Lentil stew keeps well in the refrigerator for up to one week. Stew can also be frozen in an airtight container for up to three months.

Ravioli Minestrone

1 package (7 ounces) refrigerated three-cheese ravioli
2 teaspoons vegetable oil
2 carrots, chopped
1 stalk celery, chopped
1 medium onion, chopped
6 cups water
1 can (about 15 ounces) chickpeas, rinsed and drained
1 can (about 14 ounces) diced tomatoes with garlic and onions
3 tablespoons tomato paste
1 teaspoon dried basil
1 teaspoon dried oregano
¾ teaspoon salt
¾ teaspoon black pepper
1 medium zucchini, cut in half lengthwise and sliced (about 2 cups)
1 package (10 ounces) baby spinach

1. Cook ravioli according to package directions. Drain; keep warm.

2. Meanwhile, heat oil in Dutch oven over medium-high heat. Add carrots, celery and onion; cook, stirring occasionally, about 5 minutes or until vegetables are softened.

3. Stir in water, chickpeas, tomatoes, tomato paste, basil, oregano, salt and pepper. Bring to a boil; reduce heat and simmer 15 minutes or until vegetables are tender. Add zucchini; cook 5 minutes. Stir in spinach; cook 2 minutes or just until spinach wilts. Stir in ravioli.

Makes 8 servings

 To further reduce the cost of this recipe, substitute dry pasta such as bowtie for the refrigerated ravioli.

Spicy Squash & Chicken Soup

1 tablespoon vegetable oil
1 small onion, finely chopped
1 stalk celery, finely chopped
2 cups cubed butternut squash (about 1 small)
2 cups water
1 can (about 14 ounces) diced tomatoes with chiles
1 cup chopped cooked chicken
2 teaspoons chicken bouillon granules
½ teaspoon ground ginger
¼ teaspoon salt
⅛ teaspoon ground cumin
⅛ teaspoon black pepper
2 teaspoons lime juice

1. Heat oil in large saucepan over medium heat. Add onion and celery; cook and stir 5 minutes or just until tender. Stir in squash, water, tomatoes, chicken, bouillon, ginger, salt, cumin and pepper.

2. Cover; cook over low heat 30 minutes or until squash is tender. Stir in lime juice. *Makes 4 servings*

 tip Use leftover roast chicken or cook 2 boneless chicken thighs and chop to make 1 cup.

Hearty Vegetable Stew

1 tablespoon vegetable oil
1 cup chopped onion
¾ cup chopped carrots
3 cloves garlic, minced
4 cups coarsely chopped green cabbage
3½ cups coarsely chopped red potatoes (about 3 medium)
1 teaspoon salt
½ teaspoon dried rosemary
½ teaspoon black pepper
2 cans (about 14 ounces each) chicken broth
1 can (about 15 ounces) white beans, rinsed and drained
1 can (about 14 ounces) diced tomatoes
Grated Parmesan cheese (optional)

1. Heat oil in large saucepan over medium-high heat. Add onion and carrots; cook and stir 3 minutes. Add garlic; cook and stir 1 minute.

2. Add cabbage, potatoes, salt, rosemary and pepper; cook 1 minute. Stir in broth, beans and tomatoes; bring to a boil. Reduce heat to medium-low; simmer about 15 minutes or until potatoes are tender. Sprinkle with cheese, if desired. *Makes 6 to 8 servings*

Cuban-Style Black Bean Soup

2 teaspoons vegetable oil
1 small onion, chopped
1 cup thinly sliced carrots
2 jalapeño peppers,* seeded and minced
2 cloves garlic, minced
1 can (about 15 ounces) black beans, undrained
1 can (about 14 ounces) chicken or vegetable broth
1/4 cup sour cream
1/4 cup chopped fresh cilantro
4 lime wedges (optional)

*Jalapeño peppers can sting and irritate the skin, so wear rubber gloves when handling peppers and do not touch your eyes.

1. Heat oil in large saucepan over medium heat. Add onion, carrots, jalapeños and garlic; cook and stir 5 minutes.

2. Add beans and broth; bring to a boil. Cover; reduce heat to low. Simmer 15 to 20 minutes or until vegetables are very tender.

3. Ladle soup into bowls; top with sour cream and cilantro. Serve with lime wedges, if desired.

Makes 4 servings

 tip | This soup will be chunky. For a smooth texture, process the slightly cooled soup in a food processor or blender to the desired consistency. For a thick yet somewhat chunky texture, process only half of the soup.

One-Dish Favorites

99¢ or LESS

Cajun-Style Beef and Beans

- ¾ pound ground beef
- ¾ cup chopped onion
- 2½ cups cooked rice
- 1 can (about 15 ounces) kidney beans, rinsed and drained
- 1 can (about 14 ounces) stewed tomatoes
- 1 teaspoon Cajun seasoning*
- ¾ cup (3 ounces) shredded Cheddar cheese

*Depending on the brand, Cajun seasoning may be high in sodium. Taste and adjust the seasoning if necessary.

1. Preheat oven to 350°F. Brown beef in large skillet over medium-high heat 6 to 8 minutes, stirring to break up meat. Drain fat. Add onion; cook and stir 3 to 5 minutes or until onion is translucent.

2. Combine beef mixture, rice, beans, tomatoes and Cajun seasoning in 2- to 2½-quart casserole. Bake, covered, 25 to 30 minutes, stirring once during baking. Remove from oven; sprinkle with cheese. Let stand, covered, 5 minutes before serving.

Makes 6 servings

Cajun Seasoning: Place 5 tablespoons ground red pepper, 3 tablespoons black pepper, 3 tablespoons onion powder, 3 tablespoons garlic powder, 3 tablespoons chili powder, 1 tablespoon dried thyme, 1 tablespoon dried basil or parsley flakes and 1 tablespoon ground bay leaves in a medium bowl. Stir until the spices are mixed well. Stir in ½ cup salt, if desired. Store in tightly sealed container.

Cha-Cha-Cha Casserole

1 tablespoon vegetable oil
1 pound ground turkey or chicken
1 cup chopped onion
3 cloves garlic, minced
1 tablespoon chili powder
1 teaspoon salt
1 teaspoon ground cumin
1 can (about 14 ounces) diced tomatoes with green chiles
1 can (about 15 ounces) corn, drained
1 can (16 ounces) refried beans
1 can (about 4 ounces) diced green chiles, drained
2 cups (8 ounces) shredded Mexican cheese blend
2 cups crushed tortilla chips
½ cup sliced green onions (optional)

1. Preheat oven to 375°F. Spray 8-inch square baking dish with nonstick cooking spray.

2. Heat oil in large skillet over medium-high heat. Add turkey, onion, garlic, chili powder, salt and cumin; cook, stirring to break up meat. Stir in tomatoes; cook about 10 minutes or until liquid evaporates.

3. Spoon turkey mixture into prepared baking dish; top with corn, beans and chiles. Sprinkle with cheese and crushed chips. Bake 30 minutes; let stand 5 minutes before serving. Garnish with green onions, if desired.

Makes 6 servings

 **New Mexican Pork Stew**

1½ pounds boneless pork shoulder, cut into 1-inch pieces
2 medium baking potatoes or sweet potatoes, peeled and cut into pieces
1 cup chopped onion
1 cup frozen corn
1 can (4 ounces) diced green chiles
1 jar (16 ounces) salsa or salsa verde (green salsa)
2 teaspoons sugar
Hot cooked rice (optional)
¼ cup chopped fresh cilantro (optional)

Slow Cooker Directions

1. Place pork, potatoes, onion, corn and chiles into 4-quart slow cooker. Combine salsa and sugar in small bowl. Pour over pork and vegetables. Stir gently to mix.

2. Cover; cook on LOW 6 to 8 hours or on HIGH 4 to 5 hours or until pork is tender. Serve stew with rice and cilantro, if desired.

Makes 6 servings

Note: When preparing ingredients for the slow cooker, cut into uniform pieces so that everything cooks evenly.

 Always taste the finished dish before serving. Salt, pepper, a little vinegar, lemon juice, minced fresh herbs such as cilantro or dried herbs such as cumin, chili powder or oregano perk up the flavor of a slow-cooked dish.

Zesty Chicken & Rice Supper

1 pound boneless skinless chicken thighs, cut into
 1-inch pieces
1 can (28 ounces) crushed tomatoes
2 large bell peppers, chopped
1 cup uncooked rice
1 small onion, chopped
1 cup water
1 package (about 1 ounce) taco seasoning
1 teaspoon salt
1 teaspoon black pepper
 Shredded Cheddar cheese (optional)

Slow Cooker Directions

1. Combine chicken, tomatoes, bell peppers, rice, onion, water, taco seasoning, salt and black pepper in slow cooker; mix well.

2. Cover; cook on LOW 6 to 8 hours or on HIGH 3 to 4 hours. Garnish with cheese, if desired. *Makes 4 servings*

 Keep the lid on! The slow cooker can take as long as 30 minutes to regain heat lost when the cover is removed. Only remove the cover when instructed to do so by the recipe.

Ham and Swiss Penne Skillet

8 ounces uncooked penne pasta
2 slices bread, torn into pieces
5 tablespoons butter, divided
3 tablespoons all-purpose flour
2¾ cups milk
6 ounces ham, diced
1 cup (4 ounces) shredded Swiss cheese
1 cup frozen corn, thawed
¾ cup frozen peas, thawed
½ cup finely chopped green onions
Salt and black pepper

1. Cook pasta according to package directions. Drain well; keep warm.

2. Place bread in food processor; pulse to form coarse crumbs. Melt 2 tablespoons butter in large skillet over medium heat. Add bread crumbs; cook and stir 2 minutes or until golden. Transfer to plate; set aside.

3. Melt remaining 3 tablespoons butter in same skillet over medium heat. Add flour; whisk 2 minutes or until smooth. Gradually add milk, whisking constantly to blend. Cook and stir 4 minutes or until slightly thickened. Add pasta, ham, cheese, corn, peas and green onions; stir gently to blend. Season with salt and pepper. Cook 4 minutes or until heated through. Sprinkle with bread crumbs. Serve immediately.

Makes 4 servings

Mexican Casserole with Tortilla Chips

1 pound ground turkey
1 can (about 14 ounces) stewed tomatoes
1 bag (8 ounces) frozen bell pepper stir-fry mixture, thawed
¾ teaspoon ground cumin
½ teaspoon salt
¾ cup (3 ounces) shredded sharp Cheddar cheese
4 ounces tortilla chips, slightly crumbled

1. Cook turkey in large nonstick skillet over medium-high heat until no longer pink, stirring to break up meat. Add tomatoes, pepper mixture and cumin. Bring to a boil. Reduce heat to medium-low. Cover; simmer 20 minutes or until peppers are tender.

2. Remove from heat. Stir in salt; sprinkle evenly with cheese and chips.

Makes 4 servings

Variation: Sprinkle chips over the bottom of a casserole. Spread cooked turkey mixture evenly over the chips. Top with cheese.

 For a taco salad, place ½ cup meat mixture over 2 cups chopped lettuce. Top with chips and cheese.

Italian-Style Shepherd's Pie

1 pound potatoes, peeled and quartered
2 to 3 tablespoons chicken broth
3 tablespoons grated Parmesan cheese
1 pound ground beef
½ cup chopped onion
2 teaspoons Italian seasoning
⅛ teaspoon black pepper
2 cups sliced yellow summer squash
1 can (about 14 ounces) diced tomatoes, drained
1 cup frozen corn
⅓ cup tomato paste

1. Preheat oven to 375°F. Spray 2-quart casserole with nonstick cooking spray.

2. Combine potatoes and enough water to cover in medium saucepan. Bring to a boil. Boil, uncovered, 20 to 25 minutes or until tender; drain. Mash potatoes, adding enough broth to reach desired consistency. Stir in Parmesan cheese. Set aside.

3. Brown beef and onion in large skillet over medium-high heat 6 to 8 minutes, stirring to break up meat. Drain fat. Stir in Italian seasoning and pepper. Add squash, tomatoes, corn and tomato paste; mix well.

4. Spoon mixture into prepared casserole. Pipe or spoon potatoes over top of casserole.

5. Bake 20 to 25 minutes or until meat mixture is bubbly. Let stand 10 minutes before serving.   *Makes 6 servings*

Southwestern Corn and Pasta Casserole

    1 tablespoon vegetable oil
    1 red bell pepper, chopped
    1 onion, chopped
    1 jalapeño pepper,* minced
    1 clove garlic, minced
    2 cups frozen corn
    1 can (4 ounces) sliced mushrooms, drained
    ½ teaspoon salt
    ¼ teaspoon ground cumin
    ¼ teaspoon chili powder
    8 ounces elbow macaroni, cooked and drained
    1 tablespoon butter
    1 tablespoon all-purpose flour
 1½ cups milk
    1 cup (4 ounces) shredded Monterey Jack cheese
        with chiles
    1 slice bread, torn into ½-inch pieces (optional)

*Jalapeño peppers can sting and irritate the skin, so wear rubber gloves when handling peppers and do not touch your eyes.

1. Preheat oven to 350°F. Grease 3-quart glass baking dish.

2. Heat oil in large skillet over medium-high heat. Add bell pepper, onion, jalapeño and garlic; cook and stir 5 minutes. Add corn, mushrooms, salt, cumin and chili powder. Reduce heat to low; simmer 5 minutes or until corn thaws. Stir in macaroni; set aside.

3. Melt butter in large saucepan over medium heat. Stir in flour. Gradually stir in milk. Cook and stir until slightly thickened. Gradually stir in cheese. Cook and stir until cheese melts. Add macaroni mixture; mix well.

4. Spoon into prepared baking dish. Sprinkle with bread, if desired. Bake 20 to 25 minutes or until bubbly. Let stand 5 minutes before serving. *Makes 4 servings*

Honey-Glazed Chicken

1 can (20 ounces) pineapple chunks in juice
1 tablespoon cornstarch
2 tablespoons honey
1 tablespoon Dijon mustard
½ teaspoon ground ginger
¼ teaspoon red pepper flakes
1 tablespoon vegetable oil
1 pound boneless skinless chicken thighs or breasts, cut into pieces
1 green or red bell pepper, cut into pieces
3 cups hot cooked rice

1. Drain and reserve pineapple. Combine pineapple juice and cornstarch in small bowl; stir until smooth. Add honey, mustard, ginger and red pepper flakes; mix well.

2. Heat oil in large skillet over medium-high heat. Add chicken; cook and stir 5 minutes or until browned. Add bell pepper; cook and stir 3 minutes. Stir in reserved pineapple and juice mixture.

3. Bring to a boil. Reduce heat to medium-low. Simmer 5 to 8 minutes or until chicken is cooked through and sauce thickens. Serve with rice.

Makes 4 servings

 Boneless skinless chicken thighs are a great value and can be used in place of boneless skinless breasts in many recipes. Chicken thighs can be almost half the price per pound of chicken breasts.

Hearty Burritos

¾ pound ground beef *or* 15 ounces chorizo, cut into bite-size pieces

1 can (about 15 ounces) red beans, rinsed and drained

1 can (about 14 ounces) diced tomatoes

1 green or red bell pepper, cut into 1-inch pieces

1 cup chicken broth

1 can (about 5 ounces) corn, drained

½ teaspoon ground cumin

½ teaspoon ground cinnamon

5 to 6 flour tortillas, warmed

1½ cups hot cooked rice

Shredded Monterey Jack cheese

Slow Cooker Directions

1. Brown beef in large skillet over medium-high heat 6 to 8 minutes, stirring to break up meat. Drain fat.

2. Place beef, beans, tomatoes, bell pepper, broth, corn, cumin and cinnamon into slow cooker; mix well. Cover; cook on LOW 6 to 8 hours.

3. Spoon filling down centers of warm tortillas; top with rice and shredded cheese. Roll up and serve immediately.

Makes 5 to 6 servings

 Brown ground meats before cooking in a slow cooker. Browning not only adds flavor but also helps to reduce the fat. Just remember to drain off the fat in the skillet before transferring the meat to the slow cooker.

Mom's Meat Loaf

¾ cup tomato sauce, divided

4 tablespoons chunky salsa, divided

I egg

½ teaspoon black pepper

½ cup old-fashioned oats

½ cup finely minced onion

⅓ cup canned mushroom stems and pieces, drained and
    chopped (optional)

I clove garlic, minced

½ pound ground beef

½ pound ground turkey

1. Preheat oven to 350°F. Line jelly-roll pan or shallow baking pan with foil. Spray with nonstick cooking spray.

2. Mix ½ cup tomato sauce, 3 tablespoons salsa, egg and pepper in medium bowl. Stir in oats, onion, mushrooms, if desired, and garlic.

3. Crumble ground beef and ground turkey into large bowl; mix lightly to combine. Add tomato mixture; mix well.

4. Transfer meat mixture to prepared pan; shape into 4×8-inch rectangular loaf. Mix remaining ¼ cup tomato sauce and 1 tablespoon salsa in small bowl; spread over top of meat loaf.

5. Bake 55 minutes or until cooked through (165°F). Let stand 5 minutes before slicing.

Makes 4 servings

Edamame Frittata

2 tablespoons vegetable oil
½ cup frozen shelled edamame
⅓ cup frozen corn
¼ cup chopped onion
5 eggs
¾ teaspoon Italian seasoning
½ teaspoon salt
½ teaspoon black pepper
¼ cup chopped green onions (about 4)
½ cup (2 ounces) shredded Monterey Jack cheese or
    crumbled goat cheese

1. Preheat broiler. Heat oil in large broilerproof skillet over medium-high heat. Add edamame, corn and onion. Cook and stir 6 to 8 minutes or until onion is brown and edamame is hot.

2. Meanwhile, beat eggs, seasoning, salt and pepper in medium bowl. Stir in green onions. Pour egg mixture over vegetables in skillet. Sprinkle with cheese. Cook over medium heat 5 to 7 minutes or until eggs are set on bottom, lifting up mixture to allow uncooked portion to flow underneath.

3. Broil 6 inches from heat about 1 minute or until top is puffy and golden. Loosen frittata from skillet with spatula; slide onto small platter. Cut into wedges to serve.   *Makes 4 servings*

 tip | A frittata is an omelet with the ingredients mixed into the eggs. Frittatas are economical because almost anything appetizing can be combined with the eggs. Use about one to two cups filling for every four to five eggs. Frittatas are also a versatile menu item because they can be served for any type of meal, including appetizers. And, they even taste great at room temperature.

Swiss, Tomato and Turkey Patty Melt

1 pound ground turkey
1 medium green onion, finely chopped
½ packet (0.4 ounce) ranch salad dressing mix
1 tablespoon vegetable oil
2 slices Swiss cheese, halved diagonally
1 medium tomato, diced
4 hamburger buns (optional)

1. Combine turkey, green onion and salad dressing mix in medium bowl; mix well. Shape into 4 patties.

2. Heat oil in large nonstick skillet over medium heat. Cook patties 14 minutes or until cooked through (165°F), turning once.

3. Remove skillet from heat. Top each patty with cheese. Cover. Let stand 2 to 3 minutes or until cheese melts. Top each patty with tomatoes. Serve with buns, if desired. *Makes 4 servings*

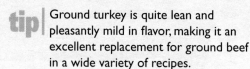

tip | Ground turkey is quite lean and pleasantly mild in flavor, making it an excellent replacement for ground beef in a wide variety of recipes.

Taco-Topped Potatoes

4 small or medium russet potatoes
¾ pound ground beef
½ (1¼-ounce) package taco seasoning mix
½ cup water
1 cup diced tomatoes
¼ teaspoon salt
2 cups shredded lettuce
½ cup (2 ounces) shredded sharp Cheddar cheese
¼ cup finely chopped green onions (optional)
½ cup sour cream

1. Scrub and pierce potatoes with fork. Microwave potatoes on HIGH 6 to 7 minutes or until fork-tender.

2. Meanwhile, brown beef in large nonstick skillet over medium-high heat 6 to 8 minutes, stirring to break up meat. Drain fat. Add seasoning mix and water; stir to blend. Cook 1 minute. Remove from heat.

3. Combine tomatoes and salt in small bowl; mix gently.

4. Split potatoes almost in half and fluff with fork. Fill with equal amounts of beef mixture. Top with equal amounts of tomatoes, lettuce, cheese and green onions, if desired. Serve with sour cream.

Makes 4 servings

 tip | What's for dinner? Baked potatoes with toppings are a family favorite meal for lunch or dinner. Try other toppings such as broccoli and Cheddar cheese sauce.

X Veggie Dish

Black Bean Cakes

1 can (about 15 ounces) black beans, rinsed and drained
¼ cup all-purpose flour
¼ cup chopped fresh parsley or cilantro
2 tablespoons plain yogurt or sour cream
1 tablespoon chili powder
2 cloves garlic, minced
1 tablespoon vegetable oil
½ cup salsa
1 pouch (about 6 ounces) Spanish rice mix (optional)

1. Place beans in medium bowl; mash with fork or potato masher until almost smooth, leaving some beans in larger pieces. Stir in flour, parsley, yogurt, chili powder and garlic. Shape bean mixture into 8 patties.

2. Heat oil in large nonstick skillet over medium-high heat. Cook patties 6 to 8 minutes or until lightly browned, turning once. Serve with salsa and rice, if desired. *Makes 4 servings*

tip | This recipe also makes 4 burger-sized patties. For a menu variation, make bean burgers and serve on whole wheat buns with your favorite toppings.

Sausage and Cheese Pizza

Nonstick cooking spray
1 can (about 14 ounces) refrigerated pizza crust dough
1 package (about 7 ounces) turkey sausage breakfast links (7 links), thinly sliced
1 medium red onion, thinly sliced
1 medium green bell pepper, thinly sliced
¾ cup pizza sauce
Red pepper flakes (optional)
1½ cups (6 ounces) shredded mozzarella cheese

1. Preheat oven to 425°F. Spray 15×10-inch jelly-roll pan with cooking spray. Unroll crust on pan; press to edges of pan. Bake about 6 minutes or until crust begins to brown.

2. Meanwhile, spray large nonstick skillet with cooking spray. Add sausage; cook and stir over medium-high heat 2 to 3 minutes. Add onion and bell pepper; cook and stir about 5 minutes or until bell pepper is crisp-tender.

3. Spread pizza sauce evenly over crust; top with sausage mixture. Sprinkle with red pepper flakes, if desired. Top with cheese. Bake 7 to 10 minutes or until crust is golden brown and cheese is melted. Cut pizza into 8 pieces to serve.   *Makes 4 servings*

 Make pizza for pennies quickly and easily at home. For the crust, either make the dough, buy frozen or prepared dough or use pita bread or tortillas. Topping possibilities are endless. Utilize tiny bits of leftovers such as grilled vegetables. With a little bit of cheese and a few ingredients, pizza is a simple way to enjoy a home-cooked meal.